T0144947

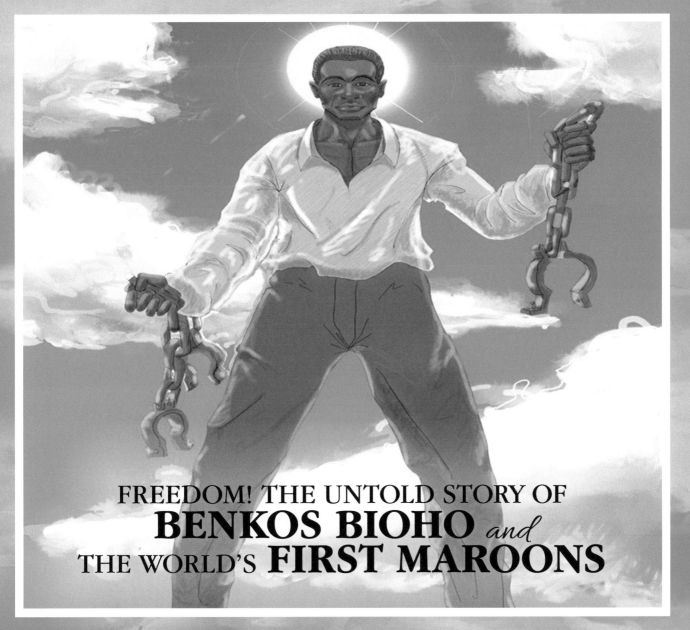

Kofi LeNiles & Dr. Kmt Shockley

FREEDOM! THE UNTOLD STORY OF
BENKOS BIOHO *and*
THE WORLD'S **FIRST MAROONS**

A TRUE STORY

AuthorHouse™
1663 Liberty Drive
Bloomington, IN 47403
www.authorhouse.com
Phone: 1 (800) 839-8640

© 2019 Kofi LeNiles & Dr. Kmt Shockley. All rights reserved.

No part of this book may be reproduced, stored in a retrieval system,
or transmitted by any means without the written permission of the author.

Published by AuthorHouse 01/02/2019

ISBN: 978-1-5462-7393-6 (sc)
978-1-5462-7394-3 (hc)
978-1-5462-7392-9 (e)

Print information available on the last page.

Any people depicted in stock imagery provided by Getty Images are models,
and such images are being used for illustrative purposes only.
Certain stock imagery © Getty Images.

This book is printed on acid-free paper.

Because of the dynamic nature of the Internet, any web addresses or links contained in this book may have changed
since publication and may no longer be valid. The views expressed in this work are solely those of the author and do not
necessarily reflect the views of the publisher, and the publisher hereby disclaims any responsibility for them.

authorHOUSE®

I was born into a royal family in a small village in Africa.

As I grew older, one day I was walking in the village to go visit my grandmother.

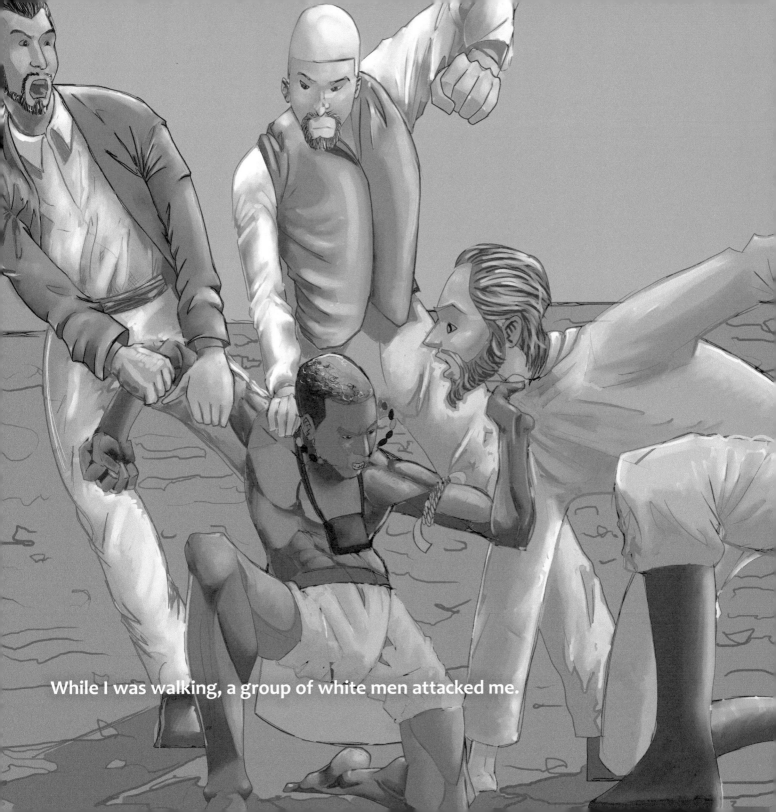

While I was walking, a group of white men attacked me.

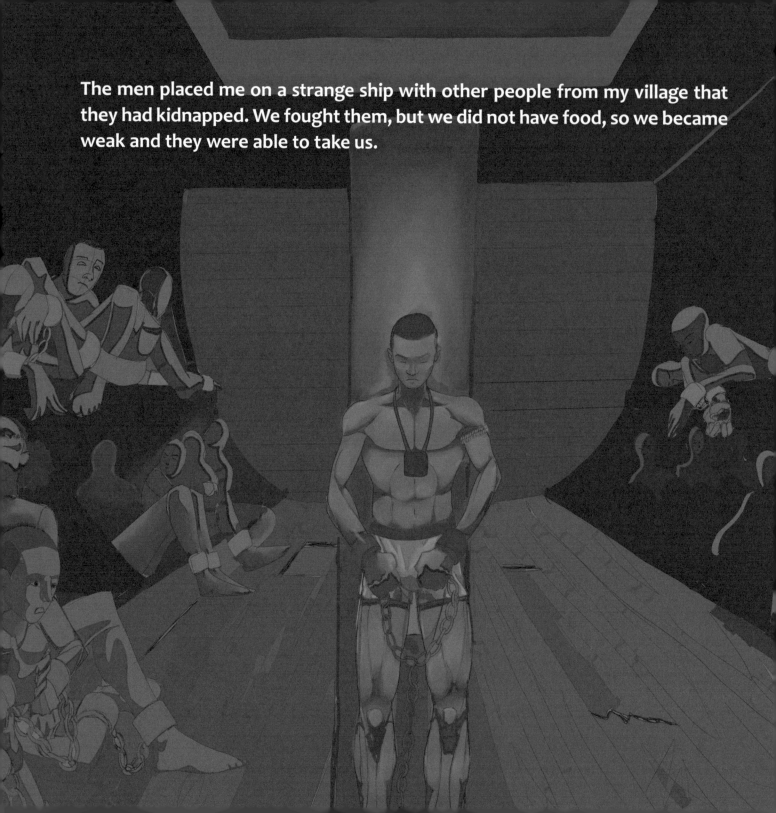

The men placed me on a strange ship with other people from my village that they had kidnapped. We fought them, but we did not have food, so we became weak and they were able to take us.

My parents went looking for me, but they could not find me in the village because I was on the boat with the mean men.

When I arrived in the new land, I saw thousands of people who look like me that had also been captured. One man who spoke my language told me, "they call this place New Grenada." He said, "New Grenada is the worst place on earth." New Grenada is now called Colombia. It is a country in South America. Colombia is known for its coffee, agriculture, emeralds and its music.

The people who captured us would not let us practice our own culture, sing our own songs, or talk to one another. I missed my village back in Africa.

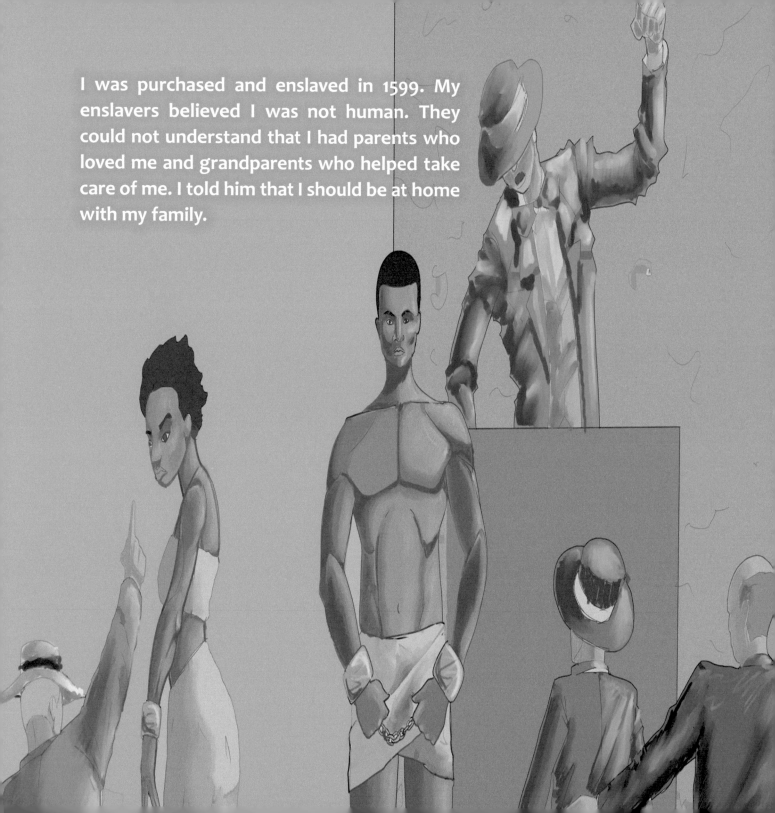

I was purchased and enslaved in 1599. My enslavers believed I was not human. They could not understand that I had parents who loved me and grandparents who helped take care of me. I told him that I should be at home with my family.

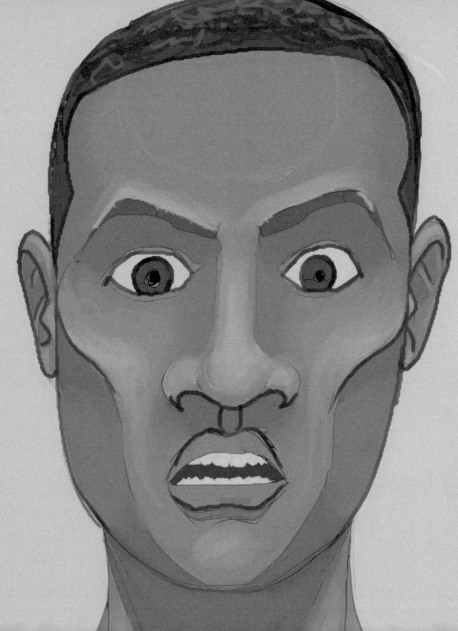

As I got older, I had to remember the things that my parents and teachers taught me. What the white man did not know is that ... I remembered!

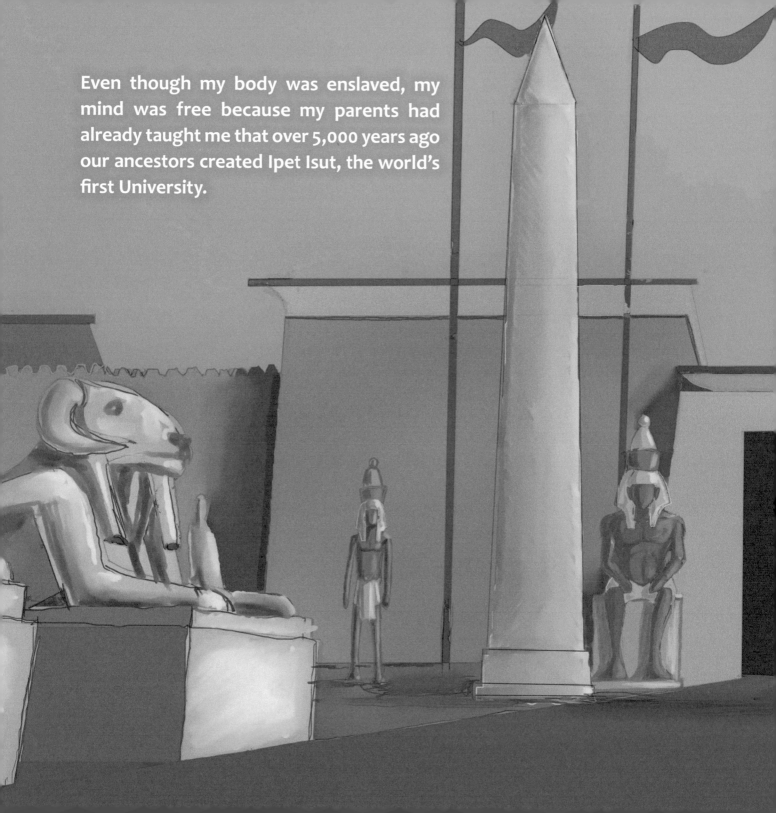

Even though my body was enslaved, my mind was free because my parents had already taught me that over 5,000 years ago our ancestors created Ipet Isut, the world's first University.

My parents had already taught me that my ancestors built the first great civilization and it was called Kemet.

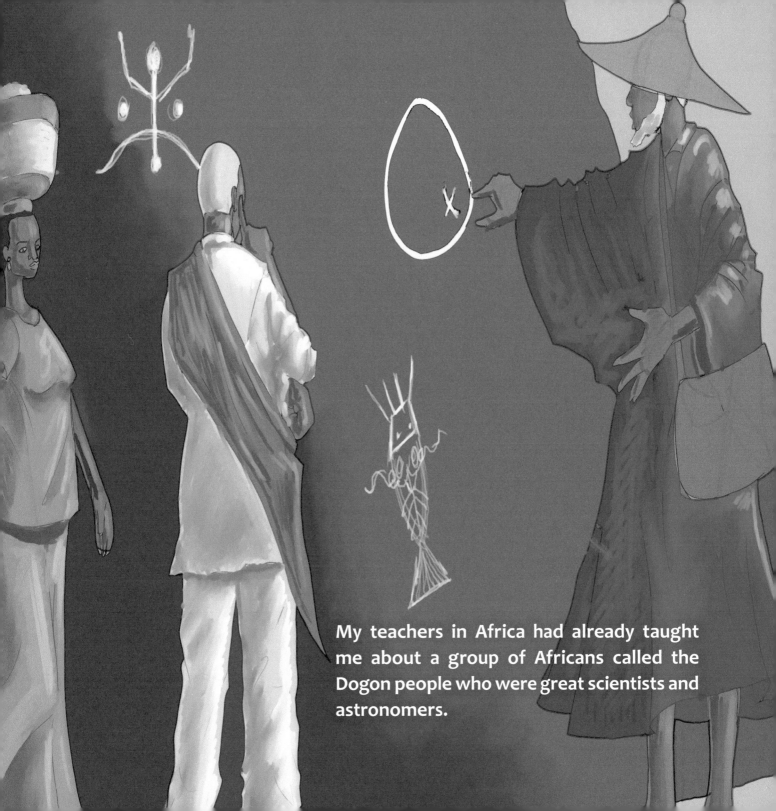

My teachers in Africa had already taught me about a group of Africans called the Dogon people who were great scientists and astronomers.

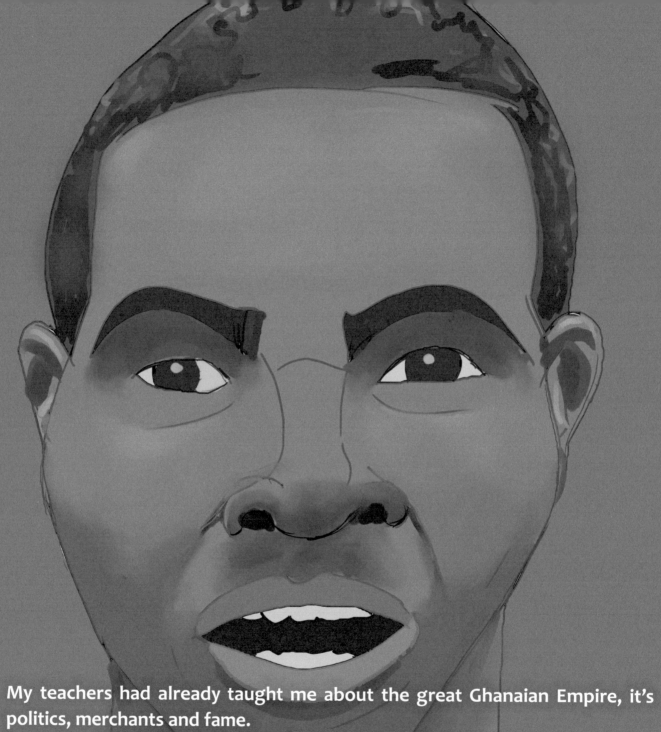

My teachers had already taught me about the great Ghanaian Empire, it's politics, merchants and fame.

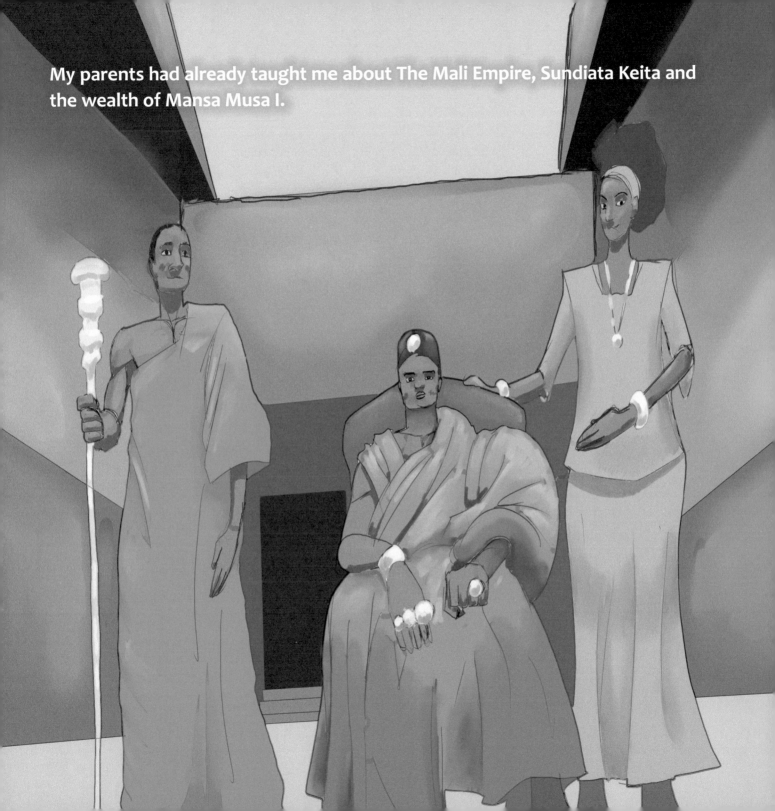

My parents had already taught me about The Mali Empire, Sundiata Keita and the wealth of Mansa Musa I.

My parents had already taught me about the Songhai Empire and I learned that Timbuktu was an education capital where many people came to Africa to learn about science and other subjects.

And even though they captured me, I remembered the sound of the drum, the smell of Africa, and I knew that I must get free...

... So, In 1603 I freed myself and others, we escaped, and together we created a community called Palenque. In Palenque, we practiced our African way of living.

We also fought and freed people from other plantations, and we accepted those who were able to free themselves and find us!

Ever since I created Palenque in 1603, many people have sacrificed their lives to protect this land and its people. Deep within the core of our land are the spirits and memories of those who sacrificed.

When Africans escaped from plantations and created villages where they were free, those places were called Maroon Villages. My family and I lived in the Maroon village that I created called San Basilio de Palenque.

Palenque still exists! My children's children and their children continue to live in Palenque with other families. Palenque Still Lives On as a place where we are free!

Printed in the United States
By Bookmasters